Dot-com Secrets

A Playbook to Grow Your Company Online with Sales Funnel

By

George Stallion

All trademarks and brands within this book are for clarifying purposes only and are owned by the owners themselves, not affiliated with this document.

Table of contents

Introduction

Human beings have been designed in such a way that they have the tendency to learn each and every day. The business sector has always been a very interesting spot to learn several of the sales terms. While being a business man you need to be very careful on how you are dealing your clients and what your services towards them are. To get your sales scale high you need to provide high quality services and should have the tricks and techniques to handle your clients cleverly.

Honesty can lead you way up in your game but trust me only honesty will not be enough when your aim is sky high. You need to learn all the terms and skills related to business to get your company to the exact desired spot you had once dreamed of. In this book you will get all that you need to learn to become a successful online businessman.

This book is majorly a playbook that will help you know how to grow your company's presence online with the help of sales funnel. Many of you will not be familiar with the term sales funnel. Well, no need to worry because you are exactly where you need to be. In this book, you will be able to not only learn what sales funnel is but the different phases, building blocks, various types of sales funnel as well. Sales funnel is the marketing strategy that you use when you want to increase your sales. Getting knowledge regarding all these terms is not enough. So, we will give you a detail regarding managing your sales funnel that will help you in the days to come.

The secret formula to success in your business dealings has also been discussed in this book with the help value ladder method. You will learn the technique behind creating a value ladder and the importance of value ladder for any successful business. There are many benefits of this ladder that have been mentioned later in the chapters below.

No business can succeed without targeting their main audience, the individuals who would prefer buying from them. You will learn how to attract your target audience towards you and your role as an entrepreneur. Finding your targeted audience in the crowd can be tough tasks. So, do not worry as you will learn this specific technique as well after reading this book.

Have you ever thought of the term online traffic? Well, if no, then you need to go through all the little details regarding it. Managing your online traffic is pretty important for an online growth. So, it is time to grow online with the help of this amazing book. Do not need to stress any further as we are here to help you out of the hell hole you have been. Start reading now, and thank me later!

Chapter 1: Introduction to Sales Funnel

The sales funnel is an idea that is utilized to outwardly depict the business cycle from introductory prompts to last conclusion. It utilizes the picture of a channel where the open doors are dropped into the pipe and experience the strainer towards each stage. The open doors that do not make it to the last stage are portrayed as the broken channel where they are taken out from the pipe and fall by the wayside. Then again, the open doors that are changed over pass through the channel and into the compartment. The sales funnel is a useful representation of the probability of the leads being converted and hence, it has become quite popular among managers and sales and marketing personnel.

The objective of any e-commerce vendor is to expand the quantity of deals they make. However, this can be a troublesome assignment without a system set up. This is the place where deals channels; a high-level showcasing procedure comes in. Deals pipes are characterized purchasing measures that shippers can use to direct their possible leads through the cycle. And they can be a great thing to have if you are also looking to increase Search Engine Results Page (SERP) rankings and improve your site's established customer journey.

1.1 What is a Sales Funnel?

If you have ever attempted to sell anything, at that point you must have realized how hard it may be. You may make a deal, yet arriving at where you can produce standard income is extreme. Effective organizations do not simply make deals to a great extent. They make deals reliably and with sufficiently high volume that they can serenely recruit full time representatives. They realize that regardless of having customary costs, they will be beneficial.

A sales funnel is a bit-by-bit measure that permits you to bring your potential client one bit nearer to your offer and a purchasing choice through a progression of advertising activities like robotized messages, recordings, articles and greeting pages that will do the selling for you. For example, the sales funnel for any coffee shop may begin when you see a bit of their showcasing some place. You might be driving home one day and you see a coffee bulletin. Seeing an organization's branding lets potential clients begin getting acquainted with the brand.

At home, when you are sitting in front of the TV at night, you may see a coffee business on TV. The business may show you how the espresso is made. It could likewise show individuals appreciating the espresso and being more gainful at work. The following morning, as you will work, you stroll by a coffee shop and somebody gives you a flyer publicizing a "buy one, get one free" espresso offer. You choose to head inside and request a coffee espresso unexpectedly. The individual at the checkout counter inquires as to whether you need a treat with your request. Their treats look scrumptious so you state yes. They give you your treat and two espressos. They put a sticker on the subsequent espresso saying for your #1 colleague. While most standard people probably will not understand it, they are buying items or administrations as a result of sales funnel. Sales funnels are utilized to sell everything including data items, administrations and actual items that you see each day.

When deciding to grow a business, many people struggle with how to market their business. Most aspiring business owners have the following two options:

1. Continue to rely on hope marketing. Hope marketing means waiting around for referrals and word of mouth.

Or going to networking events and talking to random people in the hopes that you will meet a potential customer. Basically, business men who take this approach sit around and hope that business comes their way.

2. Take the time to actually build a system that attracts the right leads and turns them into paying customers. Winning companies have figured out how to acquire customer at profit and scale. The best way to do that is through a sales funnel.

Businesses that take this approach identify their target customer. They figure out where and how to reach them. These businesses also have a plan for cultivating these leads and turning them into paying customers. They might also have a plan to get them to buy more products or services and to systematically refer even more leads.

Which of these approaches do you prefer? Do you want to continue relying on external factors that are outside of your control and waiting around for business to come to you? Or would you rather take control of your destiny by building a step-by-step system that attracts the right leads and converts them into paying customers.

1.2 Different Phases of a Sales Funnel

While most customary people probably will not understand it, they are buying items or administrations due to sales funnels. Sales funnels are utilized to sell everything including data items, administrations and actual items that you see each day.

While there are lots of words used to describe different sales funnel phases, we are going to go with the four most common terms to explain how each stage works as a consumer goes from being a visitor to a prospect to a lead to a buyer.

A guest lands on your site through a Google search or social connection. The individual in question is currently a possibility. The guest may look at a couple of your blog entries or peruse your item postings. Eventually, you offer the person in question an opportunity to pursue your email list. By chance that guest rounds out your structure, the person turns into a lead. You would now be able to market to the client outside of your site, for example, by means of email, telephone, or text or every one of the three.

It is easy to remember the four sales funnel phases by the acronym AIDA: Awareness, Interest, Decision, and Action. These four phases represent your prospective customer's mindset. Each phase requires a different approach from you who is the marketer, because you do not want to send the wrong message at the wrong time. It is kind of like a waiter asking you what you want for dessert before you have even ordered drinks and appetizers. Let us look at each phase in the sales funnel in more detail.

Awareness

This is the second at which you first grab a purchaser's eye. It very well may be a tweet, a Facebook post shared by a companion, a Google search, or something totally different. Your prospect customer gets mindful of your business and what you offer. When the chemistry is just right, consumers sometimes buy immediately. It is a right-place, right-time scenario. The consumer has already done research and knows that you are offering something desirable and at a reasonable price.

More often, the awareness stage is more of a courtship. You are trying to woo the prospect into returning to your site and engaging more with your business.

Interest

When customers arrive at the interest phase in the sales funnel, they are doing investigative, examination shopping, and thoroughly considering their choices. This is an ideal opportunity to dip in with unbelievable content that encourages them, however does not offer to them. In case you are promoting your item or administration from the earliest starting point, you will turn off prospects and pursue them away. The objective here is to set up your ability, help the customer settle on an intelligent choice, and offer to help them in any capacity you can.

Decision

The decision phase of the sales funnel is the point at which the client is prepared to purchase. The individual in question may be thinking about a few choices ideally, including you. This is an ideal opportunity to make your best offer. Whatever the case, make it so irresistible that your lead can't wait to take advantage of it.

Action

At the lower part of the sales funnel, the client demonstrations are there. The individual in question buys your item or administration and turns out to be important for your business' environment. Because a customer arrives at the lower part of the channel, however, does not mean your work is finished. Activity is for the shopper and the advertiser. You need to give a valiant effort to transform one buy into 10, 10 into 100, etc. As such, you are focusing in on client maintenance. Express gratitude for the purchase, invite your customer to reach out with feedback, and make yourself available for tech support, if applicable.

All the phases mentioned above are equally important while making a suitable sales funnel for your business plan.

1.3 Building Blocks of a Sales Funnel

Sales funnels are composed of building blocks. These building blocks make a sales funnel complete and effective. Following are the twenty-three building blocks:

- Quiz
- News
- Blogs
- Articles
- Pop-ups
- Squeeze-pops
- Squeeze-page
- Free account
- Exit pops
- Webinar Registration
- Free shipping
- Trial
- Tripwire
- Self-liquidating offer
- Straight sale
- Bamps
- On time offers
- Affiliate recommendations
- Down sales
- E-mails
- Presell page
- Video
- Free + Shipping

1.4 Various Types of Sales Funnel

Searching for the kinds of sales funnel that get additionally paying clients? There are various sorts of sales funnels for a wide scope of items, administrations, and objectives. Yet, which type do you pick? To be effective in advanced showcasing, you need to prepare and pick the sorts of sales funnel that will work for your business. We will show you eight sorts of online deals channels that are demonstrated to work and get paying clients. We will additionally show you where to discover these kinds of sales funnels so you can begin and expand your business today.

1. **Free Plus Shipping Sales Funnel**

The Free plus Shipping Sales Funnel offers something in the $5 to $7 value range. These kinds of sales funnels are additionally extremely viable to get your guests to begin purchasing from you. Despite the fact that you may at first lose cash toward the front, the objective of this funnel is to get a purchaser. When you have a paying client, you would then be able to move them to upsells to build your benefit toward the back.

Books, health items, and low-ticket consumables function admirably with these sorts of funnel. Here, guests are pulled in to yours sales funnel by means of the free in addition to transportation offer. The principal page is a business page with a video or pictures of your offer. You at that point direct your guests to a transportation page for their email address and conveyance subtleties.

They at that point move to an installment stage for the postage charge. By chance if a guest leaves prior to paying, you can charm them back utilizing computerized messages. If you do not mind note, it is essential to be forthright with this delivery cost on the business page. It is simply ethical to do as such. If you do not, your clients will leave your sales funnel and stay away forever. After the installment page, guests are offered an upsell. At last, guests are taken to a thank you page.

These sorts of sales funnels are demonstrated to chip away at individuals or traffic that is unfamiliar to you. They are okay for the purchaser. They likewise function admirably on the grounds that individuals will in general purchase an upsell when they have just paid a little for something with a great deal of significant worth.

2. Continuity Sales Funnel

The Continuity Sales Funnel is a type of funnel to get visitors to sign-up and pay regularly for access to content or a service. It is also called a membership sales funnel. These types of sales funnels typically provide recurring income every month.

Here, visitors are attracted to a landing page with a free trial, or very low $1 offer to get them to sign-up. Once on your email list, you can direct them to a full membership funnel via a payment page. These kinds of sales funnels are great to generate leads on the front end. But they are most profitable on the back end. With the right content or service, they can easily convert leads into full paying consumers and members.

1. Webinar Sales Funnel

The Webinar Sales Funnel gets visitors to sign-up and attend a live webinar. This type of sales funnel is great for selling training, coaching, or course related products. Webinars are now one of the best ways to deliver your sales presentation to anyone in the world. They are typically broadcast live but can be recorded. They can also be paid for or free.

In this kind of funnel, visitors are attracted by a free webinar and land on a registration page. In exchange for a name and email address, they are directed to a date and time confirmation page. Automated emails remind your new leads of the upcoming webinar. They also help to build interest and excitement.

After viewing the webinar, your leads are offered upsells. This could be a premium paid webinar, or webinar related products of higher value.

Leads are then taken to a payment stage (not shown), and finally a thank you page. If your leads leave during (or after) the webinar, and without buying the upsells, you can reach out to them with emails to woo them back. As a bonus, you can record a live webinar and resell it again and again using an automated webinar sales funnel. These types of funnels are extremely profitable and work very well for products and services.

2. High-Ticket Sales Funnel

The High-Ticket Sales Funnel gets visitors to apply before they can buy premium products from you. These types of sales funnels allow you to better qualify your potential clients. Also called an application sales funnel, high-ticket funnels work best for selling high-end coaching packages, and consulting services.

With a very selected offer, it gets rid of objectives, and pre-frames your prospect to the higher cost. It also gets them to prove to you why you should take them on as a client. Visitors are attracted to a case study page by a high-end product or service. Here, a video explains the results your clients can achieve with coaching from you.

Having watched the video, you then guide them to an application form page. Here, they have to complete a questionnaire to pre-qualify for your services. This helps to increase interest and demand for your service. It also helps you to qualify your leads

3. Consultation Sales Funnel

The Consultation Sales Funnel gets visitors to speak to you directly about your products and services. These types of sales funnels are great for generating leads. They are also a good opportunity to convert visitors into paying customers immediately.

This kind of funnel works for products or services that require a conversation before purchase. For example, information products, personal training, and products with multiple add-ons.

Visitors are attracted to a registration page via the offer of a free consultation. On signing up, a free one-on-one consultation is arranged. Shortly thereafter, you consult with your new lead via phone or a Zoom/ Skype video call. After the consultation, emails promote your full priced products and services. Each email offer directs new leads to a sales page, and then a payment page for purchase. Emails are also used to offer new paid consultations. Of course, with this type of sales funnel, you can also convert leads into paying customers during the free consultation.

4. Product Launch Sales Funnel

The Product Launch Sales Funnel builds anticipation before people can buy from you at a specific time. As the name implies, these types of sales funnels are for physical products. But they can also be used for services. These funnels are excellent at building a sense of scarcity and urgency to buy your products. Done in the right way, these kinds of funnels can drive up an insatiable demand prior to launch.

Visitors, leads and existing customers are attracted to a registration page by your new product offer. Here, they register to get exclusive access to watch your upcoming live launch. They are also signing up to exclusively pre-order too. Shortly after registration, a series of three emails is sent to your registrants. Each email has a link to a sales page with a different pre-launch video for your product. Each video helps to build more awareness, interest and desire for the launch.

The final email is the launch invitation. Here, registrants watch and participate in the live broadcast. This then gives them access to a payment or reservation stage to pre-order and buy your product. If registrants drop out during the launch, or after watching but before ordering, emails are used to woo them back.

5. Self-Liquidating Offer Sales Funnel

The Self-Liquidating Offer Sales Funnel is a type of sales funnel that covers its own traffic costs. It is able to 'liquidate' its advertising expenses using a higher priced front-end product. This means that you are technically getting higher quality leads for free. And, if you can do that, then all your future upsells on the back end of the funnels are pure profit. As you will see from the stages above, this type of sales funnel is very similar to the opt-in lead generation funnel. Visitors are attracted by a lead magnet on a landing page. A free guide, report, or video is the offer in exchange for their email address.

But, instead of waiting for an email to direct them to the funnel, here you can guide your new leads directly to a sales page with a higher priced front-end offer. The following stages are the same as the opt-in lead generation funnel. Once again, if your leads leave the funnel before payment, another series of emails guide them to return and buy.

6. Opt-In Lead Generation Sales Funnel

The Opt-In Lead Generation Sales Funnel is a type of sales funnel that every website must have. It is simple to use, and has the basic building blocks of every other type of sales or marketing funnel. It is also called a lead magnet sales funnel. As the name suggests, the goal is to get leads on the front end of the funnel. But, this type of sales funnel also converts leads into paying customers on the back end.

Visitors are attracted in to the sales funnel via a lead magnet like a free guide, e-book, or video. This will be on your website homepage, or dedicated sales funnel landing page. Here, visitors give you their email address in exchange for your free offer. You then reach out to your new leads via a series of automated emails with priced offers.

Each offer guides visitors to a sales page and then to a payment stage to buy. After paying, your new buyers are offered an upsell. This is an opportunity to upgrade, or buy an additional product. It also helps you to increase your cart value. After the upsell, your paying customers are taken to a thank you page. These types of funnels are perfect for you to grow your email list and start making sales too.

Many people make sales funnels complicated and confusing. But they do not need to be. Choosing which types of sales funnel strategy to use is easier than you think. Combining multiple or different types of sales funnels is where their true power lies. It is like bolting an extra few engine onto your rocket ship. As you build your email list, you can use multiple sales funnel types for various stages of your customers buying journey.

1.5 Frontend vs Backend Funnel

Optimizing your inbound marketing regimen for lead generation is no easy task for marketers. Doing so requires creating compelling content that resonates with your target audience, then taking the initiative to promote your content across a myriad of social media channels and web properties. But optimizing the back end what happens to convert a one-time buyer into a loyal lifetime customer is an even more special challenge.

For those unfamiliar with the terminology, the front end of the sales funnel is where you convert prospects into first-time customers, whereas the back end of the sales funnel is the part where you take one-time buyers and convert them to longer-term bigger-ticket loyal customers.

As an entrepreneur bootstrapped an e-commerce business and had to learn from scratch how to optimize the back end sales funnel of what is now a multi-million business, we can tell you that fresh leads are seldom ready to become loyal customers. If you want to increase your sales conversions, then you will need to optimize the back end of your email campaigns.

Front end sales funnel is any offer that gets another client. The sort of offer is superfluous. It very well may be a free in addition to delivery offer, a profound limited offer, and so forth what makes a difference is that there is a deal and you are catching a purchaser not simply a pick in. Despite the facts that opt in can likewise be on your front end. In one or the other case, climate you have a proposal for a deal or a select in as the initial phase in your front end, you will typically additionally have a front-end sales funnel comprising of a tripwire offer or potentially a few up sells and down sells. This is your front-end sales funnel.

Back end sales funnel is any offer that offers to a current client. Again, the kind of offer is insignificant. The significant think to learn is that this is in the back end. So, it as a rule comprises of a subsequent email grouping that supports the purchaser and moves them onto another offer, which thus is really another funnel with up sells and ruins behind that, or a high-ticket value ladder.

What this simply means is that you make more money by selling additional products to the same customer than you make on the initial front-end sale. In fact, the top marketers are actually making no money on the initial first sale. Sometimes they are even going in the hole, losing money on that first sale.

In the offline world this is known as a loss leader. This is why you see those deep discount deals on Black Friday. The brick-and-mortar business hope is that the super bargain deal will bring you in the store and you will wind up buying other things while you are there. The only marketer however takes this to the extreme. Where the offline brick-and-mortar store will limit the up-front deal to a limited number of times online there is no limit or there is a fake limit.

1.6 Effectively Manage Your Sales Funnel

A sales funnel is an inverted pyramid that draws potential customers through a company's sales process. As the name indicates, it is wide at the top because customers with all level of engagement enter and eventually the strongest leads are channeled to the bottom to be turned into successful sales.

Successful sales are characterized by identifying potential leads that will convert to purchasing customers. Because of the extremely large number of people showing initial interest and the relatively smaller number of people actually looking to buy, it is a difficult process to correctly identify and focus your efforts on the right people.

This is where an efficiently managed and effectively created sale funnel acts as a filter. When it flows smoothly, a sales funnel can offer tremendous benefits to the business. Conversely, if the funnel becomes needlessly complicated, it can actually become a hindrance to the process and slow things down.

It therefore remains imperative to ensure that the sales funnel is long enough to act as an effective filter, but not so long that it becomes too complex and starts leaking prospects from the side. An ideal funnel will smoothly channel prospective leads downwards while horizontally removing the rest to avoid clogging the entire passage. Among other things, a sales funnel can be kept relevant through the following activities. Following are the things you should do:

- **Target Qualified Leads**

There are numerous examples where those answerable for the highest point of the funnel pass, everything being equal, to the business groups as opposed to appropriately qualifying them. This is a vital mix-up as a larger part of those leads will never transform into deals. By having them all in a pool to focus on, the business group will wind up investing fundamental energy, exertion and assets into focusing on somebody who will never transform into a fruitful deal.

All things being equal, proprietors of the top and center pieces of the funnel should be prepared to appropriately recognize just those leads that can be transformed into deals, regardless of whether now or sometime in the future. Since not all leads require a similar data and backing, a more modest pool of leads will permit the business group to offer expanded items and administrations to meet a wide range of prerequisites.

- **Remove Roadblocks**

Ensure that no leads move on a level plane inside the pipe. All things being equal, they should have the option to move generally easily downwards, with just a periodic interruption to address concerns and assemble more data.

If it is taking too long to convert leads into sales, then the funnel and the processes built into it need to be carefully evaluated to eliminate any unnecessary steps.

By asking pointed questions as to why the delays occur, you can identify if it is a problem outside the funnel such as access to decision makers or a fault in the marketing communications. But more often than not, it will also lead to an identification of redundant process steps within the channel as well.

It is important to note that steps should not be removed just for the sake of simplification. If an intelligent process study is not undertaken, it will result in incomplete or missing steps that may result in a loss of leads. Any steps that add no value or require additional actions that are not necessary should be targeted for removal only.

- **Use a Customer Relationship Management Technique**

A straightforward however successful Customer Relationship Management application will enhance the funnel and permit the business group to monitor various clients and their particular prerequisites. It can likewise help mechanize and improve certain cycles and make the funnel work considerably more easily. Yet, it is the key here to pick a framework that is straightforward and does not add further multifaceted nature to the cycle.

Do not simply focus in on the final product and measure that as a triumph or disappointment. All things considered, center around the result at each stage inside the funnel. Maybe every move was done well in an occasion where a deal did not wind up occurring. Maybe all some unacceptable moves were made yet a deal happened in any case. Each stage should be estimated and surveyed to comprehend that it has viability inside the cycle just as to guarantee that the business group is following convention as it should.

Do not continually endeavor to chip away at creating prompts add more traffic into the funnel. It is not sufficient to simply make a great deal of leads.

All things being equal, it is similarly significant, if not more to deal with dealing with these leads through positioning, arranging, supporting and following up on them. Deals results can improve definitely by focusing in on the current leads that show the most potential than on expanding their amount.

Try not to get self-satisfied with regards to consistent learning and preparing. These activities are not only for those new to the business game. All things considered, all degrees of the business group regardless of their degree of involvement need occasional boosts to permit them to keep up to date with the most recent procedures and to learn by imparting information and encounters to other people.

Chapter 2: The Secret Formula to Success

There is a mystery equation to reliably surpass your business objectives, however as you may expect, it is difficult. Fortunately, the vast majority can do it, if they decide to. Set a significant standard and genuinely focus on it. It begins with the objectives themselves. What are you ready to focus on? It is safe to say that you are prepared to take the way to submitted execution and drop your reasons?

If not then quit perusing. Assuming this is the case, let us experience the means to progress. Investigate your allocated objective and set your objective. Try not to go for 100%. Stretch yourself to 110% or 120%. That way if you miss the mark, you will even now hit or surpass your objective.

Focus on improving your genuine win-rate. The vast majority and associations have a roughly 25% success rate, or less. That implies a 75% lose rate. We as a whole know the round of not revealing every one of your business occasions to diminish the executives' desires and make your success rate look higher.

Preclude awful deals openings quicker. First — begin relinquishing a few deals openings. However, by chance that you just have a 25% success rate you are pursuing an excessive amount of unfit business. This can be difficult; however, it is critical to your prosperity. Do not cling to things that have a low likelihood of being won. Work more intelligently and begin excluding business.

Try not to rely on others to fill you deals channel. The subsequent stage is basic; you need to fill the channel. Try not to depend on marketing for drives as this should turn into an individual mission. Showcasing may give you some certified leads, however by chance that you will surpass your objective; you need to assume responsibility for filling your sale. Begin conversing with contacts and draw in individuals.

Target individuals inside your records to share thoughts. The more you do this, the greater open door you will have. To be protected, your funnel ought to have no under 4x of the estimation of your month to month or quarterly objective. In this way, gear up and hit the business exercise center. Get the telephone, begin sending messages, request and follow up on references. The world can change for you in as meager as one month on the off chance that you finish.

Evaluate your revenue pipeline realistically. Focus on the reality of what is in your pipeline. Be honest to yourself. Do not count on winning opportunities that have a probability of less than 70%. Evaluate each opportunity as clinically as you can. Use whatever sales intelligence tools you have. Saying you will do something and doing it are two different things, and the biggest key to making your words become a reality is planning. If there are opportunities you are committing to, be sure you invest the time to plan how you will win it.

To be a high performer, year after year set higher goals for your target. Commit to it and plan. Focus on improving your win-rate. Evaluate and disqualify opportunities faster. Be honest with yourself. Do not count on Marketing to fill your pipeline. Use your sales tools to realistically evaluate your pipeline monthly. Top performers will be top performers because they are willing to do what others are not and enjoy what others cannot. The secret formula works, but it is not magic. Transparency, commitment, planning, and discipline are the secret to your success.

2.1 Value Ladder Method

A value ladder is a lineup of offers that increase in price and value that meet people where they are on their journey to become a customer; from initial awareness to their final decision to buy your premium offerings. It is an effective way for you to build trust and maximize the lifetime value of each customer. The value ladder allows you to cater to your client's needs no matter where they are at. At the very bottom of the value ladder, you create free content that visitors to your website can download in exchange for their email address. As clients ascend the ladder, the value level increases, as does the cost to play.

Clients who are ready to make the next level of commitment can. You are covering all bases and making sure you provide the most value to your clients. The result is that you increase your impact and your revenue. If you only have one price or offering you could be leaving money on the table at both ends of the ladder.

They are generally examined with regards to deals channels and it can at times seem like: "get however much cash out of them as could be expected for as long as possible!" But a business' first basic is not benefit, it is to get and keep clients; benefit is the outcome. So, it is imperative to make that your essential target while making a value ladder. A value ladder, when executed accurately, is really interlinked with your brand methodology. You can utilize them to construct trust and eventually, move brand dedication.

It is easy to forget that most of your customers who see your marketing messages are not going to sign up instantly.

There is no magical formula that can persuade someone to whip out their credit card and purchase a premium offering if they are just not ready. Enter the value ladder. It is a way to meet people where they are in their decision-making process and readiness to commit.

The goal of any branding strategy is to communicate the reasons why customers should choose you instead of all their other options. Along the way, your job is to provide value and earn their trust in order to help them make that decision. When businesses forget that potential clients are going through this process, they do things like drop a bulleted list of capabilities on their services page and call it good.

What happens is, all the people who are just becoming aware they need you, researching their options, and gathering up the information they need to make that final decision. A value ladder, in contrast, takes prospective clients by the hand from the very first interaction and walks side by side with them as they grow to trust you.

2.2 Creating a Value Ladder

A value ladder is essentially a strategy to delineate your items or administrations arranged by worth and cost. Thus, the lower part of the value ladder would be your most economical, or perhaps free offer. This is the thing intended to get your clients in the entryway to get the joy of working with you, even on the least support level.

Preferably, a client will ascend the value ladder, so whenever they have purchased a passage item or administration, they would keep on buying more costly and important things from you. This permits somebody to go into working with you at generally safe, check it out, and proceed down the way on the off chance that they like it. A value ladder could even be beginning with a gift to catch their eye and get a foot in the entryway by offering something significant.

The ladder is not just about cash, it is tied in with making a client experience. Consider it along these lines: suppose 100 individuals select in for a gift, at that point 50 use it, love it, and need the following stage and you represent the following proposal to them that is a more modest speculation level, possibly 25 will finish and fixate on that and be anxious to do what is next. By chance, your offers are impasses without welcomes, you are leaving cash and impact on the table.

Try not to wrongly create your greatest, the most significant mark course directly out of the doors. Consider what your ideal client would require first, before they get to the huge kahuna. At that point what? What else might you be able to enhance? Lead them on the way to that huge item or administration as opposed to beginning with the biggest conceivable offer you can consider.

It is really accepted that the best benchmark for a value ladder is a gift. What better or more powerful approach to get somebody in the entryway than offering them something of significant worth for definitely no cost? It is generally suggested that item-based organizations offer a delicious markdown in return for your client's email address. For training, administration, or data-based organizations, a gift asset containing the best 10% of your data is an astounding method to get your optimal customers captivated and ready to hand over their email address. They will promptly think if that is the thing that he is parting with for nothing, it cannot be envisioned how important his paid assistance or content is.

It is preferred to generally share such gifts close by content or blog entries that cover comparative points as a spring up or footer to wrap up the post since it is definitely realized that the reader is keen on the theme and likely needs to learn significantly more.

The main thing to recollect for gifts is to keep them brief, forthright, and result-driven. Presently, you do not need to guarantee or attempt to get 57 significant outcomes for your crowd, yet they should leave the gift with something that they can promptly apply to their life and business to improve it.

When you have a Value Ladder, you have to have multiple steps, thus multiple values. Think about the services you provide and arrange them in ascending order so that you have a Value Ladder. Know the journey you want your customer to make before you approach them. Know how you can hook them into your sales funnel by understanding the ascending value of the products or services that you offer. So, you can see how from offering free content that is informative and useful, you can develop a customer base of clients with an ascending value to you as a business. And it all started from the free stuff because that got you into your sales funnel.

You probably will not have an arrangement of administrations; you may very well have one help or item that you sell or exchange. Consider how you can increase the value of your current portfolio by maybe adding additional things for which you charge more. You may have a Do-It-Yourself, a Done-For-You, an Inner Circle, a Mastermind. Consider the various ways you can separate your current contribution. Make a rundown of each assistance and property a monetary incentive to every component. Remember your entrance level, free administrations. You are probably going to require those to get your clients into your business funnel in any case.

At the highest point of your value ladder goes your top notch offering; the most important help or item you can give. It is probably going to be the situation that few out of every odd client who moves up your value ladder get to the top; paying for your exceptional contribution. Yet, by chance that you have expanded the lifetime of your relationship, assembling more income on route, at that point it is justified, despite all the trouble.

One of the most helpful components of making a value ladder is that it rapidly turns into a model of your business. It permits you to perceive how your client enters your business funnel and how they become a paying client. It gives you an overview of your business making your occupation of selling that business simpler in light of the fact that you have a reasonable excursion for the client to follow. Your employment at that point starts to be the manner by which to get individuals to join your funnel in any case.

2.3 Importance of Value Ladder Method in Online Growth

A value ladder, referred to as a brand ladder or marketing ladder is a group of offerings that increases in both price and value as you move from left to right. It is usually depicted with a set of stairs. A value ladder can do so much for you and it is really a must-have for any business owner. By implementing a value ladder, you are able to increase a customer's Life Time Value, LTV. Providing lower-cost items that build in value as cost increases allow you to build trust with your audience early in the customer journey and still make some money along the way.

Additionally, you are still meeting the customer needs and adding value, even at the lower level offers. Most value ladders work best when immense value is given even in the early steps. This allows you to show your worth to clients and build trust. But let us dive in a little more.

A value ladder is not tied in with crushing cash from individuals and encouraging them maximize a master card to two.

That is not the purpose of a value ladder, despite the fact that a great deal of showcasing specialists out there will let you know that it is. It is tied in with expanding the quantity of clients and offering some benefit proportionate with that cost at the same time fabricating trust as they travel through the various periods of the customer venture. In this way, you need a value ladder since it will build the quantity of customers and the lifetime estimation of the normal client. It will additionally help you produce cheerful clients.

With new organizations and new businesses becoming quicker than dandelions during a pre-summer shower, expanding deals and making sure about clients might be troublesome. One technique that numerous effective organizations use is to part with something that makes every potential client's life simpler and encourages them to settle on a decent choice. Would vehicle vendors have deals in the event that they did not part with some mileage during the test drives? Indeed, even retail locations part with certain items when clients are permitted to take a stab at dress; from suits to shoes to perfumes.

There are two sorts of individuals on the planet; individuals who are foolhardy and individuals who are long term arranged. Limited individuals need to make a benefit immediately. Then again, individuals with long term vision and business insight comprehend that to totally dominate the contenders, you give away things or time for free in order to get people interested, and then monetize downstream. That is the place where the value ladders come in.

The biggest hurdle between your start-up and the potential customers is trust. People do not know about the quality of your product or service; they do not know if you will be able to deliver the promised service or product in a timely manner. They do not even know if you are a genuine or fly-by night business. That is why initially giving away something valuable is an important strategy.

When these multibillion-dollar organizations are happy to part with something significant to get individuals to connect with their administrations, for what reason do you believe that, without offering any financial or non-money related value upfront, you have a possibility of winning against your rival who does? However, the extraordinary news is that most organizations do not do this. Check out your industry, and check whether you can discover any individual who is giving value upfront to the clients. The odds are thin.

Throughout that client journey, "clients to be" will touch various parts of your value ladder steps required to move them from prison to paradise. This is an important point, as what your audience and ideal client really desire is to find internal relief from the problem they are experiencing. Even if and when your customers show up with an external problem, which they will, the underlying problem you need to meet is internal and is found in the look, sound, and feel of your audience.

The brain science of purchasing and client conduct is a very intriguing field, however not in the ballpark of this conversation. In any case, it has been indicated that to get a client, to pay as much as possible there should be trust. In other words, individuals vote with their cash. In the event that they are not paying you, they are not prepared to cast a ballot or they vote against you. You need to place clients in a circumstance where they feel great spending cash since going through cash prompts spending more cash, which leads to two things. Furthermore, this is significant.

It prompts a superior result for your customer eventually, on the grounds that there is more incentive as they spend cash. Your free offer will never help them similarly that a paid bulldog offer will help them.

You know this and where it counts, they know this, yet some portion of the client venture is strolling through the way toward really understanding this.

You are able to meet people where there are if you have ever seen conceptualizations of the marketing funnel, there is a whole slew of different versions. Most marketing funnels will be broken into at least three parts. Awareness or some other word that depicts a similar concept. Next, you have consideration and research. And finally, a decision is made by your customer. With a value ladder, you create offers at different levels, which help the buyer journey along.

Having tiered offers in the value ladder allows people to jump in or to taste the product. At a minimum cost or investment to themselves, in the end, this helps move potential clients through the customer journey. One thing that is interesting about the funnel image provided above is if you turn it on its side, you can build a value ladder out of it.

2.4 Benefits of Value Ladders

By the time you reach the actual buying stage, you will only have a few people left. It is, therefore, a journey that every visitor to your website goes through before they fully become customers. You need to grow your business bigger and collect more revenue by working towards widening the top of the ladder and creating engaging content that will lead to conversation.

The primary concern of a value ladder is to give your customers room to make decisions on whether to buy or not. This decision will depend on how your content is able to convince them. Every business, whether small or big, needs marketing value ladder. Here are some of the benefits your business will get from a value ladder.

1. Prediction and Accountability

A value ladder is helpful in showing you how many people have moved down to the final stage which is the purchase. This way, you can easily tell who made a purchase and who did not. By predicting your sales, you are able to improvise new and existing strategies towards improving your marketing efforts.

With a value ladder, you also say goodbye to confusions and reaching out to leads blindly. You can know your best sources of leads, the best-selling products, and the location of most of your customers among many things. This way, you know where to focus most of your marketing efforts and if applicable, know which salesperson to reward more for exceeding expectations.

2. Identify Problems

In the business world, there are so many errors that you can do without realizing it. Most of these mistakes affect your customers. Through your customers, you can identify any problem and tackle it before it goes out of hand.

A marketing value ladder will help you identify these problems better. For instance, when a potential customer exits the value ladder at any given stage, you can trace the root cause of the exit. This way, you can take necessary measures to correct it and also create a better marketing strategy.

3. Minimum Errors

Value ladders are mostly automated; hence you will not need human interventions most of the time. Lack of human intervention also means fewer errors. A business with the least errors is likely to minimize losses or unnecessary expenditure. So, if your sales team is prone to making mistakes, it is high time you work with a value ladder and save your business from falling.

What makes a value ladder so powerful is the use of a back end email autoresponder. Once you have acquired a new email through the use of a squeeze page, you can then send your email prospect through what is known as an email ladder. Sending the customer multiple follow up emails helps in the "dating" process and helps your reader get to know you and what you are about. Not all visitors who enter their email through your landing page will purchase from you initially.

4. Easier Marketing

The most challenging part of running a business is the marketing aspect. A value ladder makes it easier by giving you an accurate view of the number of leads that enter your ladder and not those who are converted at the final stage. You can use these to calculate the number of extra efforts you need to put so that you get more leads to enter your ladder.

Once you know this, you can wisely invest your money in the appropriate lead sources and platforms and get the returns for your investments. Marketing ladders, much like any other form of lead generation requires testing. You want to focus and pay close attention to what landing pages get the most engagement and conversions. Determining the best offer or lead magnet used to generate leads to introduce new visitors into customers. You really want to focus on these various aspects of your ladder for optimization to ensure higher lead and sales conversions.

5. Consistent Sales

As a business person, you need to have consistent revenue flow to be able to run your business effectively. Ups and downs in revenue stream can mess up your business and prevent you from planning ahead because you do not know what the future holds.

A value ladder allows you to bring in new clients and filter them towards the end of the ladder. You can market your business without putting in too many efforts and at the end come up with some customers. The customers who go through the value ladders process are likely to stick around and keep purchasing from you. This way, you get the revenue security as you continue sourcing for more.

6. Improved Conversation Rates

It is easy to get people into your website. You can attract as many people as you can and get them to subscribe to your site. However, this does not guarantee that they will make a purchase in the long run. You will start out with a wide audience, but as the process goes on, you find that most of them drop along the way. You need those who will stay to buy the products in the long run.

Those that stay are the ones who will boost your conversation rates. Building an effective marketing value ladder is similar to dating. Before you ask that special someone to marry you, you have to go through a courting process to build that relationship. You first have to introduce yourself to your ideal person based on your attraction to them. This would be the same as finding your targeted audience.

Then over time, you start to date the person in order to get to know them, what makes them stick, and what things they like and dislike to build trust. In a ladder, this would be the process of building interest with the potential customer. There has to be some interest demonstrated by the customer to consider going out on a second date with you.

The more time you take establishing a relationship with your targeted customer through the use of the value ladder, and then you can build on that relationship using email marketing as your tool. Eventually, that person that you spend time courting and getting to know will eventually feel comfortable with you and will consider marrying you, or at least buying something you are offering. Another reason why value ladder increases your conversation rates is by giving you a 360-degree view of the way every lead passes through the ladder. You get to understand what it takes to convert a customer so that you take the necessary steps.

7. Prioritize Interest of the Customers

Adopting a value ladder strategy simplifies marketing for you. By looking into the ladder, the marketers can decide on the sequence of steps they need to follow to optimize the customers' experience. Marketers can employ intelligent predictive insights to optimize the experiences of the audiences in the future.

8. Gives Life to Branding Through Powerful Storytelling

As you can tell powerful brand stories, while prioritizing the preferences of your customers to show the value preposition of your products and services, you naturally upsell your products and services. Relevant story telling not only presents the customers as the ultimate heroes in a brand's story but also helps by building a rapport by communicating a narrative that resonates with the pain points of the customers.

By developing the art of powerful story telling you can optimize the conversations by enticing and inspiring the prospects to take the right actions, at the right time, to move up the ladder.

Developing a value ladder is all about being goal oriented to sustain and win in the competitive marketplace. It is all about getting the fundamentals correct and trust me acquiring new prospects is simple but not easy. Executing a value funnel strategy helps you choose, pursue, and convert the right prospects by providing them with seamless experiences at each stage of their respective buying. So, in short, value ladders are extremely important to your brand.

Businesses have used value ladders for years and are continuing to benefit from them. If you have not embraced it yet, then you are missing out on a lot. It is difficult to get those customers who will approach your business and buy directly without passing through a process. This is even made more difficult with the digitization that has made competition more intense. Your business can only survive and thrive through a value ladder.

Chapter 3: Target Audience

A target group or in other words an intended interest group is a gathering of individuals recognized as being likely clients of a business. Target crowds share comparable segment attributes including, yet not restricted to: age, sex, financial status, training, and area. Identifying your target audience as a business can help craft marketing strategies and define your core customers. Instead of spending money and resources trying to cater to every consumer, defining a target audience allows for more intentional and personal outreach to those most likely to purchase your product or service.

The most ideal approach to discover your intended interest group is by first contemplating the particular requirements your item or administration satisfies. It is imperative to recognize the problem area, and afterward figure out who has those trouble spots. For instance, by chance that you have discovered that making sites is a problem and start a business that plans sites, your subsequent stage is discover who needs a site that would probably experience difficulty making one. In this situation, your intended interest group is likely entrepreneurs.

The more explicit you can distinguish your intended interest group's segment, the more powerful you can publicize to them. In this model, it is ideal to focus in on entrepreneurs that are probably going to be less actually solid. Rather than considering entrepreneurs as your intended interest group, you may decide to focus in on entrepreneurs over a particular age in a specific area.

By chance that your item is general in nature, you will not need to do as much statistical surveying to discover your intended interest group.

In the event that the crowd is more explicit, it is essential to accumulate information about your clients so you can limit center. One approach to gather information is to offer a unique cost or coupon code to the individuals who visit your site or business if they round out a study that catches the data you need.

Target crowds assist organizations with promoting productively as you probably are aware who your intended interest group is and how to contact them. While it is essential to reach however many individuals as could be expected under the circumstances, and it frequently seems like focusing in just on explicit portions of the populace is restricting, you need to arrive at potential customers straightforwardly.

Straightforwardly arriving at those inspired by your item or administration will eventually place more cash in your pocket. However, before you choose what your message is and how to convey it, you need to comprehend who you will get it. For individuals to get tied up with an item or administration, they need to identify with the message's tone and content. By inspiring an emotional response from somebody, an individual association is made, and trust is set up.

Suppose the objective is to offer an item to working moms. The publicizing techniques may utilize advanced and web-based media stages and may have a vivacious and compassionate tone. A superior way to deal with targeting resigned seniors is an advertising effort utilizing print promotions in papers and magazines that convey a gentler and more loosened up tone.

One drawback of a target audience is that companies may become too narrow-focused on the defined target audience that they overlook or disregard other potential consumers. Even well-researched target audiences may mistakenly exclude people who are interested in the product or service, so it is important to use target audiences as baselines, not the end-all. As your product and service offerings begin to expand, it is essential to continuously reevaluate your target audience.

As outbound promoting offers approach to inbound missions, organizations are finding the advantages of an intended interest group. By focusing on a particular choice of clients with every one of your publicizing efforts, you guarantee you are going through cash where it really matters. Advertisers see an up to 20% expansion in deals when utilizing customized content. Today's organizations realize that all messages do not necessarily resonate the same way with different groups of people. By finding and engaging your intended interest group, you improve the effect of your advertising endeavors.

The more examination you direct into your crowd, the more you may find that you do not have only one client persona to target. Numerous organizations that sell more than one item or administration additionally need to make different objective crowd profiles as well. Your intended interest group may comprise of many various examples and it will be dependent upon you to provide food your missions to those personas dependent on your objectives.

Luckily, the more you deal with your intended interest group bits of knowledge, the simpler it will be to redo your missions. The data you have will even lead you to the correct channels and procedures for sharing your message. For example, an exceptionally visual crowd may react well to an Instagram crusade.

Then again, a more established crowd may lean toward email and Facebook. Following your missions will permit you to expand on what you think about your intended interest group over the time.

If you reach out to the target audience in online campaigns you are really close to success. Targeting the right audience means better results in your activities, so for marketers, it is one of the crucial steps. Sometimes marketers are looking for audiences that are not available yet. That is why some of data providers, offer creating custom segments and target audiences tailored to client's needs. If you want to find your target audiences, try to create custom segments and reach them with personalized ads, tailored to their interests or current purchase intention.

Finally, experiment. Build basic, standard segments and use them in your campaign to check how they perform. Next, try to create a new segment, add a non-obvious attribute, build audiences based on how much they spend and offer them products that they can afford to buy. Discovering your audience, what they are looking for, what they truly need is an exciting journey. Analyze what they do, offer them personalized brand experience and measure the results. Building the right audience is not a single activity to increase the sales you need to review your target audiences and check how their expectations change over time.

3.1 Finding Your Target Market

When deconstructing the market, focusing on a small core allows you to see what is important to them, where they hang out; both online and offline and what they are exposed to. With that understanding, you can build a basic picture of their life, and flesh out your content from there.

Try not to think of keeping a targeted profile as excluding anyone, but rather keeping your messaging focused on the people who will make the most impact. Trust that everyone else will follow once you made an impression with your core market.

If you maintain a private company, possibly you have a thought of your objective market. However, an obscure thought is not sufficient to contend in the present merciless business climate. Without definite information on your objective market, you could be losing business to your rivals or passing up occasions to expand deals.

Basically, an objective market is a particular gathering of individuals you have chosen to focus with your items or administrations. It very well may be an enormous market or a specialty market. Sounds adequately straightforward, is not that so? Indeed, the idea of target markets can turn out to be considerably more convoluted on if you offer an item or administration with wide allure, or you have an assorted client base. In the event that you sell to everyone, at that point how are you expected to characterize your objective market?

In spite of the fact that target market and segment are firmly related terms, they are not tradable. Contrasted with socioeconomics, target markets will in general be a lot more extensive. This is on the grounds that, for some organizations, their items or administrations appeal to a wide scope of people. Target markets can likewise be influenced by contemplations, for example, purchasing cycles, item time span of usability and different components that may not be driven by individuals who may be keen on purchasing what you are selling. Also, advertisers regularly take the drawn-out benefit capability of an objective market into thought when building up their models and showcasing methodologies, implying that they need to focus in on the master plan.

Socioeconomics, then again, are subsets of an objective market that share specific ascribes. For instance, numerous TV promoters intentionally focus on the desired 18-35 age segment. That does not really imply that individuals who are more seasoned than 35 fall outside of the objective market; it just methods that they are important for an alternate segment. At the end of the day, you can consider target markets as an assortment of socioeconomics that might be keen on your item or administration. All in all, presently we discover somewhat more about what an objective market is, how would you approach distinguishing one for your current business?

One of the initial steps to recognizing an objective market for your business should be to take a long, hard glance at the individuals who as of now purchase from you. Regardless of whether your present clients appear to be an assorted pack, the odds are very acceptable that they will share at any rate a couple of regular qualities. By chance that they do not, maybe a shared interest is the consistent idea. When you start to recognize shared traits between your normal clients, you can start to utilize this data to refine your current client base into an objective market.

When investigating objective business sectors, it is imperative that you start expansive, yet become progressively granular as you progress. For instance, you may begin by recognizing mortgage holders as a possible segment, however then drill down further and find that mortgage holders with more established youngsters, procuring a specific yearly pay who work in a specific area are your best clients. This degree of granularity makes it easier to tailor your messaging to appeal to these individuals, even if your customer base is actually much broader.

One of the most well-known slip-ups made by organizations of all sizes is an inability to perceive that not every person finds a way into perfect minimal segment boxes. For instance, you can utilize sex as a beginning stage when leading investigation into your current client base. Be that as it may, sex is not generally twofold and a few people, for example, transsexual people, may not be effectively sorted into thin socioeconomics. It is essential to be as inclusionary as conceivable when taking a look at possibly delicate socioeconomics, particularly in the symbolism and language utilized in your messaging, otherwise you risk alienating members of your community and prospective customers.

Market segmentation can help you understand how your products or services appeal to individuals across several demographics within your target market. Market segmentation typically falls into four distinct categories: Geographic, Demographic, Psychographic, and Behavioral.

Picking the correct business sectors likewise implies mixing ends with target information. This information may come from an assortment of sources. You can likewise take advantage of your organization of business partners, funders, and guides. Ask them to deliberately look at your item or administration, perhaps to the degree of attempting it for a few days or weeks. They may amaze you and consider target advertises that you could not ever have envisioned, just as creative ways for those gatherings to utilize your item

At whatever point conceivable, draw on assorted viewpoints as you fabricate your promoting endeavors. Your ultimate objective is to make it simple for your objective segment gatherings to see associations between their necessities and your item. The examination of various surges of data, just as a persistent exertion to distinguish your objective clients, can assist you with accomplishing this end and boost your return on investments.

3.2 Finding Your Desired Customers Online

If you think basically having a site with some content is sufficient, reconsider. With all the sites out there, individuals will not go to your site since it is new and sparkling. You need to go out and discover your clients on the web so you can all the more likely to market your brand, items, and administrations. Realizing how to discover clients online will bring about more site traffic and income for your business.

In the present advanced climate, discovering clients' online starts with understanding the various channels for doing as such. From upgrading your site to show up in list items to connecting with via web-based media, there are various procedures to discover clients on the web. Following are the different ways you can connect with your customers online:

1. Pay Per Click

In some instances, like social media marketing, you will be better off attracting customers through paid ads. Pay-per-click is used to get immediate web traffic and for getting quick attention and exposure to products and services that customers already know about and are actively searching for. Common pay per click strategies include paid search ads through Google Ads or banner display ads and Facebook ads.

2. Organic Social Media

Organizations can likewise rank naturally via online media; however, it is more troublesome. Web-based media stages ceaselessly invigorate their content which pushes Facebook posts and Twitter tweets down in the client's newsfeed. The farther down an update is, the more uncertain clients will draw in with that brand. To show up at the top via online media, you should present viral content on the perfect individuals at the perfect time. Ordinary posting via web-based media channels for the duration of the day can likewise expand your odds of natural web-based media achievement.

3. Organic Search

The objective of each advanced advertiser is to upgrade their site so clients can discover their site through natural hunt. Natural hunt happens when a web client types in key phrases into the inquiry bar on their internet browser. Web indexes like Google and Bing will show a rundown of sites they believe are generally pertinent to a particular hunt. Web clients will commonly tap on the sites that show up at the highest point of indexed lists.

By chance that you improve your site so it comes up in list items for specific keywords and the client navigates your site, you have pulled in them through natural hunt. Natural inquiry is useful for a drawn out computerized promoting methodology, especially for items and administrations that individuals think about and are effectively looking for.

4. Brand Referrals

In business, the idea is not what you know, however whom you know has become the inspiration driving systems administration, business improvement, and organization building. Business people and entrepreneurs simply striking out on their new undertakings depend on systems administration and references to develop their new organizations and collect brand trust and authority.

Online brand references include organizations connecting with other authentic, profoundly perceived brands to make a cross advancement association where the two organizations advance through notices or connections to the next business. Brand reference and systems administration can assemble brand awareness and authority for new organizations that need social capital, and may take any of the accompanying structures:

- Composing item surveys
- Visitor contributing to a blog
- Referencing different brands and items from outsiders
- Getting recorded on online registry locales
- Third party referencing

5. Paid Social Media

Significant online media stages have showcasing and promoting alternatives where organizations can pay to have their brand, items, or administrations included at the highest point of the page. Facebook and Instagram, for example, have paid promoting accessible. Both these web-based media stages have simple bit by bit directions so you can make advertisements very quickly. Much the same as natural online media, paid web-based media is useful for brand awareness, especially for items and administrations that individuals may not think about or look for.

6. Using Keywords

Some computerized advertisers move diverted with search engine optimization (SEO) and numerous entrepreneurs think the main part of the showcasing office's financial plan and endeavors need to go towards it. Any site, nonetheless, can profit by streamlining. The least complex approach to direct site improvement is through embedding keywords into site contents and blog entries.

Google's Keyword Planner can help you locate the best key phrases. When you have a rundown of key words you need to rank for, experience your site content and blog entries and add them where they should be. Make sure to dodge key phrase stuffing which can bring about extreme punishments by Google.

Being available online alone will not show in internet advertising achievement. To make an effective advanced showcasing system, you should know about the distinctive online channels and advertising strategies accessible to help you discover your clients on the web. There are steps that will make your internet advertising system a powerful one that drives clients and deals to your site.

7. Choosing Channels that Work for You

Buyers' personas are great at helping you figure out not only what content would best resonate with your audience, but they will let you know what online channels your audience is active on. Each channel attracts a particular crowd and has unique content styles that cater to that audience. To fully engage with your audience, you need to find out where they are online and then produce appropriate content. Be wary of digital marketing trends and consider whether those channels are popular with your business' audience.

8. Analyze Your Current Customers

By studying your present base of customers, you can more readily comprehend what pulls in them to your site. You can study existing clients severally:

- Examining, using different devices, how clients are cooperating with your site and content.
- Utilizing your web-based media stages to pose inquiries about them.
- Conveying an online study by means of email.

The data you assemble from your reviewing would then be able to be utilized to initiate your endeavors in picking up new online leads.

All the ways discussed above are essential to finding out your desired customers online.

3.3 Attracting Your Customers towards Your Company Online

In any territory, having a very much characterized promoting system is significant for your business to develop and pick-up footing as generally as could be expected under the circumstances. If you need to draw in more clients, the primary thing you need to do, clearly, is contacting them. In this way, utilizing internet, showcasing for your potential benefit is vital.

Key arranging should be continually and firmly followed, to ensure the normal result is positive, and for the most part, to guarantee that important changes are made, since various organizations require various methodologies. Most business visionaries realize it is basic to have an intensive arrangement of activities to advance a business. Nonetheless, a ton of them have questions when the opportunity arrives to choose the best procedures.

Considering there is not one ideal marketing strategy for each business, the success of any strategy depends on how it is implemented and carried out, the target audience, and, of course, the type of business. Following are some successful strategies that you can use to attract customers towards your company online:

1. Search Engine Optimization

There is no reason for having a blog with loads of fascinating substance for your crowd if your posts cannot contact them. This is the reason you need to apply SEO strategies in your posts, with the goal that your page shows up in the top spots of web crawlers, for example, Google.

Work your key words well in your writings, test titles that grab the eye of clients, compose full content and truly teach your crowd. The significant thing is to advance every one of your posts so that individuals can arrive at your content at whatever point they look for a term identified with your specialty.

2. Social Media

Web-based media, as a rule, is an extraordinary channel to speak with people in general, essentially on the grounds that basically everybody is on it. You are probably going to need to complete showcasing activities on more than one informal organization, however be mindful so as not to propel yourself too hard in spots where your crowd is not. That may really be a misuse of your time.

Remember that your informal communities additionally need to give content that increases the value of clients. So do not only promote your brand all the time.

3. Blogs

A blog is one of the best-known strategies and is used by those who want to attract customers in an organic manner online and to deliver educational and quality content. Because, when you have a blog you can write posts that answer different questions from the most basic to the most technical and that shows specific solutions for your audience.

4. Emails

Numerous individuals actually have the possibility that email is not, at this point a decent advertising methodology; all things considered, numerous clients do not try to peruse any messages sent to them. Yet, that is not what occurs, particularly if your messages have fascinating content for individuals, not simply publicizing for your items or administrations.

Make a bulletin, for instance, and send significant data by means of email to urge individuals to share their email address with you. Another choice is sending significant free assets, for example, digital books. This is a method of keeping up correspondence with your potential clients through email and furthermore to keep them drew in with your brand.

5. Sponsored Links

Supported connections are advertisements connected on different pages, typically one that is identified with your business, for which you pay to be advanced. The reason for these connections is that others looking for subjects like yours yet do not have the foggiest idea about your item or administration, can discover you on different web journals, interpersonal organizations and sites when they start following you. A showcasing technique that has satisfied clients tremendously is local advertisements. This is on the grounds that this type of paid promoting does not disturb clients' perusing experience on the pages they are on.

6. Contests

Create contests or giveaways that encourage users to buy more or bring new customers to your page. This is a marketing strategy that certain profiles use to become better known as well as gain more followers. Another type of promotion you can do is an up-sell, down-sell, or cross-sell as soon as a person finishes buying some of your products. With this, users may be interested in making another purchase on your website.

7. Use Content to Attract Backlinks

Creating quality content in various formats is a great way to attract links. However, bear in mind that it needs to be truly unique, valuable content. The kind of content you should focus on really comes down to what would be useful for your target audience.

You have plenty of options, videos, guides, infographics, spreadsheets, etc. You can even take advantage of free tools to help you out.

Getting links to your content will not only bring referral traffic, it can actually help improve your ranking on search engines. Organic traffic is fundamental to attract potential customers, especially when you think long term.

8. Webinar

Online classes are an incredible method to assemble connections and stretch out beyond potential complaints your clients may have. Indeed, whenever done effectively, it can draw in top notch leads. If you are simply beginning regarding this matter, a decent tip is to focus in on a more extensive topic. It is harder to pull in a group of people and keep them connected with in the event that you are looking at something unmistakable. Another significant hint is to make an intensive arrangement for your online course. This is not an ideal opportunity to be unconstrained. Composing content is one method of keeping away from a negative result.

9. Events

In any event, for those working web-based, all including individuals require sympathy. So, it is fascinating that you make occasions so that individuals become acquainted with and even will see you. This will cause them to acknowledge conceivable outcomes that, if just indicated on the web, could go unnoticed. If you cannot make your own occasions, attempt to at any rate take an interest in the principal ones in your general vicinity.

That way, you can chip away at your systems administration abilities and meet likely online clients, yet additionally conceivable colleagues.

10. Radio, Newspaper, Magazines, and Television

Advertising in mass media and print media depends a lot on your type of business and the communication channels your audience uses the most. In addition, you also need to plan on the expenses you will have; after all, this type of marketing strategy usually requires a larger investment.

All things considered; it does not imply that just by applying any of these tips your crowd numbers will naturally increment. With this shrewd data, you will have the option to acknowledge which methodologies are working for your business and you can focus more on those that really provide returns. Keep in mind; it is critical to quantify all that you do to ensure that your work is not in vain and that you are making a benefit.

3.4 Your Role as an Entrepreneur

A business person is a person who sets up and grows a business. They consolidate various variables of creation, for example, land, work and cash-flow to attempt to make another productive undertaking. Business visionaries are themselves a significant factor of creation and a basic part of a free market.

Business visionaries are significant in an unrestricted economy since they assist the market with reacting and changing costs and purchaser inclinations. For instance, with the ascent in the utilization of the web, a business person may see the possibility to set up another home conveyance administration which utilizes an application for purchasers to purchase. Without business people, item markets would get static and be delayed to changes in new innovation and patterns.

A successful entrepreneur may take revenue from an established business. This can cause creative destruction. This phrase is used to describe changes in the economy which in the short-term could lead to firms going out of business and job losses. However, this potential for creative destruction also creates an incentive for an established business to adapt and increase their own efficiency. For example, in response to Uber taxi services; it created an incentive for established taxi-firms to develop their own apps.

Entrepreneurs can make radical changes and introduce new technologies which significantly move on an industry. The new technological economy offers increased opportunities for entrepreneurs. Low start-up costs give entrepreneurs the potential to find new niche markets to develop. Many of the current large technological firms are relatively young and have started as small start-ups often in someone's room or garage.

An entrepreneurship is not just about price and profit. An entrepreneur may be motivated to enter an industry to offer a more ethical product or provide a service to a community. In other situations, entrepreneurs may take a risk and provide a community service such as a volunteer led railway; offering steam trains for tourists and locals. The entrepreneur can sell his new business for more than the costs of inputs or continued to grow and develop the business.

A great deal of difficult work goes into beginning and ultimately growing an enterprise. This difficult work begins with the business visionary and streams down the whole association. Although, this is a wide definition and does not generally acknowledge and feature the genuine part of business people as for their undertakings. So, to clarify it in a superior manner, allow us to separate it into points about how a business person is fundamental to a venture:

1. It is one of the most important roles of entrepreneurs to reduce the risk of an enterprise failure by bringing in people that can help the organization grow. These people can be shareholders or investors that have a stake in the company and therefore are motivated to help the company succeed.

2. In an enterprise, the business person, being the proprietor, is the greatest daring individual. He is the person who finds the money to back up his thought and furthermore the individual who is responsible despite the failure of that specific idea.

3. An entrepreneur is the person who starts the way toward making an effort by thinking of the thought for the business and arranging out how to transform that thought into a reality.

4. To guarantee that the venture sticks to lawful standards and strategies, for example, acquiring a permit is likewise the obligation of the entrepreneur. Not relating to these can mean genuine legitimate ramifications for the venture. These could be as far as monetary misfortunes for the association or something much more genuine, for example, closing down of a venture.

5. A business person obtains and distributes different assets in the association. The most significant of these assets is labor. The business person is answerable for recruiting a proficient staff to help him do his business. This is significant on the grounds that a decent administrator can take a business higher than ever, while an awful director can demolish the business. He is additionally liable for making authoritative structure and offices for a more proficient working of the enterprise.

6. Last but far from the least, the role of entrepreneurs involves acting as a forecaster. The enterprise works in a business environment and is affected by changes occurring in various aspects of this environment. It could be internal, such as strikes, machinery breakdowns; budget cuts etc. or these could be external, such as legal policy changes, political or social unrest, technological advancements, etc. An entrepreneur must be able to correctly forecast these changes and prepare the organization to deal with these changes.

Entrepreneurship is not about magnetism and magnificence. Sadly, you will likewise be serving the function of a snort in the beginning phases of your business. Information section, desk work, espresso runs and other unglamorous positions will occupy heaps of your time yet the entire time you spend will be justified, despite the trouble.

Some of these roles do not typically go away over time. You may hire more people who can take on these responsibilities, but you will still be in charge of making the final decisions and establishing the direction that your other organization leaders must follow.

That makes for a ton of weight, and for a few, the exertion will be wilder than it is worth, yet it will likewise keep your employment fascinating and give you more knowledge into the real mechanics of a business. One thing is without a doubt that entrepreneurship will transform you and change your entire course of life.

Chapter 4: Online Traffic

Much the same as traffic on a parkway alludes to the quantity of vehicles going on the road, web traffic is the quantity of web clients who travel to some random site. Every individual who signs on to a site is recorded as a visit or meeting, with a beginning and finishing point, because of in the background interchanges between a client's gadget and the site itself. Web traffic is explicit to each page of your site too, so whether you have a one-page webpage or a 50-page website, every one of those pages' traffic is designed freely of any remaining pages.

At the point when somebody visits a site, their PC or other web-associated gadget speaks with the site's worker. Each page on the web is comprised of many particular documents. The site's worker communicates each record to client programs where they are collected and framed into a total piece with designs and text. Each document sent speaks to a solitary hit, so a solitary page review can bring about various hits.

It is not just the traffic on the site's landing page that is observed. Or maybe, all portions of the site are continually checked by the worker to decide precisely the number of hits each gets. In web vernacular, a solitary visit is known as a meeting. The minutia of every meeting differs, yet each has a start and an end point.

Workers can order each demand for a page, outfitting its administrator with the data expected to decide how famous the site is and which pages get the most consideration. At the point when a web worker measures a document demand, it makes a passage in what is known as the worker log on the worker's hard drive. The log gathers entries across posterity, forming a valuable database of information that the site owner can analyze to better understand the website's visitor activity.

The achievement of a site cannot be basically decided by the measure of traffic it gets. At the point when a guest visits a site, they will regularly just bob back out of the site; the level of visits that do not change over into clicks onto a greater amount of your content is known as the skip rate. A high skip rate, or a brief timeframe on location metric frequently focuses to issues in changing over rush hour gridlock, and since most traffic has some cost, regardless of whether that cost is financial or some other asset, for example, time, it is useful for each site proprietor to augment the transformation of the traffic received on their site.

When web-based business took off during the 1990s, the measurement of web traffic was first seen as the main methods for deciding a site's prominence, as different measurements did not yet exist to check online achievement. As advanced advertisers got savvier, examining a site's exhibition turned out to be considerably more far reaching.

For an online business to thrive, it needs an enormous crowd. However, it likewise should be the correct crowd. Deciding the number of clients purchase items, generally estimated by transformation rate, shows whether an online business store is adequately selling and advertising their item contributions.

Acquiring enormous measures of traffic is eventually trivial if clients leave after only seconds. Measurements, for example, bounce rate and time on page gasp an image of how clients carry on. Site traffic is not the be all, end all of internet business execution estimations. However, it is as yet an incredible beginning stage to decide a site's omnipresence and perceivability.

Quantity will show you the number of individuals goes to your site. Quality will exhibit how your guests have drawn in with your site, including the ricochet rate, which is the number of individuals has tapped on to your page and afterward shut it down.

Lastly the cost of traffic: what amount did it cost you to get them there and accomplishing something?

Site traffic (or the quantity of guests to your site) is significant in light of the fact that the quantity of guests rises to the quantity of chances you need to add new clients. The quantity of guests to your site turns into the quantity of chances your business needs to share its brand, to give an impression, to construct relationship. The more traffic to your site, the more open doors you need to create qualified leads, to support and help take care of their concern and eventually sell your item or administration, pick up another client or customer, and keep on developing your business.

This is not just about bringing in cash. More site traffic over the long period can permit you to develop your business and not simply your benefits, grow your product offerings, recruit more representatives, open new areas, explore your resources, and grow more astounding administrations and items.

This comes down to a simple, yet sophisticated calculation. You need to have insight into the costs and expenses your business has, and how much an average customer is worth. When you know how much revenue you need then you can work backwards to calculate how much website traffic you will need to reach those goals. Basically, you are looking at your end goal and planning backwards from there.

4.1 Different Types of Online Traffic

For every online business, site traffic is the way to gauge income. Site traffic eventually produces the change in the significant business. Thus, directing people to the site turns into the essential capacity of the advertiser and entrepreneurs.

For one thing, we should discuss what really the traffic term is. Site traffic is various individuals who go to your site through different channels.

The channels can be distinctive which we will examine in detail in this book. In general, commitment, lead, change, and benefit altogether rely upon site traffic. The more traffic to the site, the more the income is.

In this section we will talk about the various sorts of site traffic. Since it is imperative to realize what the various channels to bring traffic are. A definitive point of this section is additionally telling you which channel you should focus in on. Site traffic is arranged in various sorts relying upon where the clients came from. Here, in this section, we will discuss six unique sorts of site traffic.

1. Organic Traffic

Organic or Natural traffic comes from various web crawlers like Google, Yahoo, Bing, and Yandex. Natural traffic is the best wellspring of traffic without paying any expenses. However, driving natural traffic needs heaps of Search Engine Optimization (SEO) attempts to rank for indicated watchwords. Web optimization is the assortment of methodologies to keep up the soundness of the site to rank in the SERPs (Search Engine Result Pages) by fulfilling the calculations characterized by the web crawlers.

A study shows that 66% of all online inquiries experience Google. Nonetheless, traffic from other web indexes like Bing, Baidu, and Yahoo are additionally remembered for the natural traffic metric. The measure of natural traffic relies upon the measure of substance and the general site advancement level. Natural traffic is similarly excellent on the grounds that clients go to your site since they need to. When discussing natural traffic, On-page SEO and Off-page SEO assume an incredible job.

2. Social Traffic

As you can see from its name, social traffic consists of users that have found a link to one of your pages and followed it in any of the social networks such as Facebook, Twitter, and many others. The volume of such conversions depends on how active the company is in social networks and how well it interacts with the audience and can predict its interests. By creating a strong community with highly involved and active subscribers, you can get your piece of traffic pie from platforms with millions of users.

It is a different matter that this task is not an easy one and most probably you will have to use the assistance of third-party contractors. When you start implementing your marketing strategy and actively work with social networks, most probably you will soon notice that some social platforms bring more traffic than others.

3. Direct Traffic

Direct traffic alludes to the traffic that goes to the site straightforwardly by composing the site name. Individuals go to the site without the assistance of the alluding source or channels. For the most part, direct traffic comes simply in the wake of being a renowned brand or recognizable on the lookout. Driving direct traffic has become everybody's fantasy. Getting immediate traffic needs bunches of exertion and advertising efforts since this is tied in with building up the brand in the buyer's psyche.

4. Reference Traffic

Reference traffic will be traffic that comes from different sites and different channels. More the reference to the webpage, the more the trust, and authority of the site.

Reference traffic comes when other known or obscure individuals connect the site in their blog entry which implies that you have made some sort of significant worth to them. That is the reason they are suggesting for others too. Alluding connections can be known as a backlink.

5. Paid Traffic

Paid traffic is the traffic you get from various channels like web indexes or web-based media stages by paying a specific measure of cash. Perhaps the best illustration of the paid advertisements stage is Google AdWords where organizations or people pay to Google for showing their business site on the Google Search Engine Result Pages (SERPs). Something beneficial about the paid advertisement is that you get geo-focused on promotions on a Cost Per Click (CPC) premise. You have power over the crowd of the areas which are going to show the promotions. Some other paid promotions' models are Bing advertisements, Social Media promotions like Facebook advertisements, LinkedIn promotions, Instagram promotions, etc.

6. Online Media Traffic

As the name recommends, online media traffic will be traffic that comes from Social media channels like Facebook, Twitter, Pinterest, LinkedIn, YouTube, Instagram, and other web-based media joins. The beneficial thing about web-based media traffic is that it is 100% free except if you choose to pay for advancing items or administrations. Yet, by chance that you pay to online media, at that point the traffic falls on the paid promotions traffic.

Google calculation does not consider social signs as a feature of its hunt positioning calculation. Subsequently, any connections you have based on your Facebook profile, page or gathering or Twitter will not have any huge effect on your off-page SEO endeavors aside from the traffic.

However, web-based media assumes an imperative function in directing people to the webpage. Particularly, as of late individuals invested bunches of energy in web-based media stages than some other online stage.

7. Bot Traffic

Bots are software applications developed with the intention of carrying out specific tasks. Bot Traffic is nonhuman traffic that comes to the website. In general case, the term Bot Traffic is defined from a negative perspective. But this is not the case. It all depends on what purpose the bots are being used. Google bots can be the best example to describe here. Google bot is the web crawler software used by Google, which collects documents from the web to build a searchable index for the Google Search engine. This name is actually used to refer to two different types of web crawlers; a desktop crawler and a mobile crawler.

In spite of the fact that we have discussed various kinds of site traffic and their features, the confirmed reality is that you need a wide range of traffic to your site. It is critical to focus on aggregating a wide range of traffic. There may be where you need to run paid too. There is a different advantage of running paid promotions to get traffic.

In any case, the significant actuality is if you center on delivering quality content and offer some incentive to the focused-on crowd then you can get huge loads of traffic to your site without paying single bucks. This is the place where comes the term Search Engine Optimization or SEO in short. Website design enhancement has gotten perhaps the best subject to learn in this serious world. Since there are a large number of sites and online organizations out there. By chance that you keep up appropriate SEO for your site, at that point just you will remain ahead in the serious world.

In this way, if you are an entrepreneur and your business income is profoundly affected by the site traffic then you should consider driving on the web traffic. You should realize the various systems to carry guests to your site. Thus, we trust that you have got the general thought regarding the diverse site traffic sources and their features.

4.2 Management of Online Traffic

Site traffic is the board that depicts the way of controlling the number and sort of guests to a site. Site traffic alludes to web clients who visit a site (from a work area or portable program) just as clients of local versatile applications. Site proprietors use web traffic the board answers for keeping an adequate degree of site execution and deal with the request and kind of guests who enter their site, as a rule for motivations behind reasonableness.

Expanding site traffic is a shared objective since it frequently brings about more clients and deals. However, overpowering floods in online rush hour gridlock can frequently overpower site framework. The two of the most conspicuous web-based business bottlenecks are the stock framework and installment door. These systems are often difficult to scale, and in many cases out of the direct control of the website.

A large number of these guests will be the bots that malignant entertainers use to gather up however many items as could be expected under the circumstances to exchange at gigantic markups. They utilize a gigantic volume of the bots and their automatic speed to beat all genuine clients to installment affirmation. The entrepreneur needs to isolate bots from real clients and requirements a reasonable method to appoint a request to the veritable clients who need to purchase. A virtual lounge area can help accomplish the two objectives.

Web traffic falls directly inside the web investigation measure which is a conduct assessment of the guests mind as per the kinds of sites visited by them. Site traffic is amazingly huge to measure the site sway, reach, recognize security and data transmission distribution issues and increment viewership. The more capable the site traffic, the more is the site effectiveness. The vast majority of the site traffic search is done through SEO, where web crawlers control the traffic stream and improve the website's rankings in catchphrase query items. Here are the fundamental strides to make site traffic the executives more proficient for an advanced showcasing or web-based media promoting association.

Inclusion of Backlinks in the Website

Sharing and exchanging active links on the site is a chief element of website management. The more the trading and exchange links are; the more is the scope of web traffic being attracted to the website. The links provided should be original and accurate. Links in the form of banner and pop-up advertisement and hosted content also form a considerable part of website management. Unaccredited copy pasting links and content from other websites will only bring down the corporate identity of the website and heavily mark its credibility.

Incorporate Limited Access Mechanism

A website acts like a portal to a company's inside mechanism. It is the channel of selected inflow and outflow of data being controlled by authorized personnel. A free and unhindered access to the site can lead to the entire collapse of the company's credibility and all important and confidential matters can be leaked out. Hence web traffic management must include the limited access mechanism in which only skilled and authorized recruits are permitted to operate and manage a website and control the web traffic.

Framework Management Device

System management tool enables to monitor and improve performance of the website server and along with the resource management tool it helps in adjusting the system capacity and resource allotment.

Utilize SEO Techniques

Using SEO for website traffic management with the help of search engines has numerous benefits. SEO helps the website to improve its rankings in user's search. Thus, a higher ranking leads to greater web traffic and vice versa. A simple keyword search enables the users to be connected to the web server and the traffic inflow expands.

Traffic Shaping

Traffic shaping categorizes under traffic policing. The prime aim for any website is to increase traffic that will subsequently increase its reach, popularity and yield. However, at times, excess traffic can be a major setback as it can lead to server collapse and web traffic routes being tangled. In that case traffic shaping comes handy. It allows the bandwidth packets to get delayed that minimizes the unnecessary queue in web traffic and boosts the page loading speed.

Increase Linkage to Social Media

Social media is the place where the bulk of internet users make their virtual presence known and post and share web content to boost interaction with other users. An important website management tool is to link one's website to all the available social networking sites namely Facebook, Twitter, Google +, You tube, LinkedIn, etc. This allows the web content to be more users friendly and the reach of the website to different community of users increases manyfold.

Efficient Password Protection for Websites

An efficient password protection system is a central constraint for effectual website management. This system minimizes the risk of being spammed and other server attacks. A secure and multi-step security protected password protection retains the privacy of the website and eliminates the redundant traffic overload.

Traffic Measuring

Traffic measuring helps in evaluating the type, amount and attitudes of the viewers who visit and follow the website. Different traffic monitoring tools help in managing network inconsistency and bandwidth allocation.

Nowadays, many people choose blogging as a profession. They create websites ultimately to earn money through advertising and affiliate marketing. However, the success of your advertising revenue relies on number of clicks generated from real users. This needs a lot of traffic to your site which can increase the possibility of generating revenue from advertising or affiliate sales commission. Without traffic it does not make sense for the advertisers to display ads on your site. If you are creating site for advertising revenue, it is necessary for you to understand how to manage your website traffic from the beginning.

4.3 Increasing Online Traffic for Your Company

Below are some tips and tricks that can be used to increase online traffic for your company. Follow the steps below and you will observe how effectively your online traffic increases:

1. Topic Expertise

To be seen as an expert, you can create a pillar page, which is essentially a longer blog post that broadly covers all aspects of a topic.

Then, you write cluster content, or supporting blog posts, targeting long tail keywords that show that you have covered a topic exhaustively. Focusing on long-term traffic will help you rank higher on search engines.

2. Content Repurposes

Take a well-performing blog post and repurpose that into a video. Or if you have a podcast that did really well, write up a blog post on that topic. Using content that has already performed well will continue to drive traffic to your site.

3. Organic Social Media

Natural web-based media is anything but another methodology; however, it is as yet something advertisers should focus on. Other than posting via online media stages, you can likewise utilize Instagram stories, live video, IGTV, or Facebook messenger. The key with natural web-based media is to be an early adopter of new features.

For example, Facebook is delivering a computerized lead with the help of Messenger, permitting organizations to make a mechanized Chabot experience inside Messenger to connect content proposals on your site. This is an incredible component for sending traffic to your site. It is likewise imperative to have a different web-based media methodology and utilize the correct web-based media stages not simply Facebook, Instagram, and Twitter. Stages like YouTube or Pinterest create a ton of traffic. Pinterest has extraordinary commitment rates; 66% of Pinterest clients make a buy in the wake of seeing a brand's Pins.

4. Contest and Giveaways

A straightforward method to direct people to your site is through challenges and giveaways. This can give you a snappy lift, while additionally compensating your supporters. You can have giveaways via web-based media, through your email list, or both.

5. Influencers

Influencer advertising is anything but a passing craze. Indeed, it is a spending plan and neighborly choice to direct people to your site. As indicated by Think with Google, joint efforts with YouTube influencers are multiple times more viable at driving brand commonality than those with VIPs.

6. Community Engagement

The more brand acknowledgment you have, the more traffic you will head to your site. One approach to accomplish brand acknowledgment is to be dynamic and occupied with your locale. You can actualize a commitment technique today by partaking in Facebook bunch conversations in your industry, responding to inquiries on open gathering sites, and connecting with your supporters via web-based media.

7. Guest Posting

In that equivalent vein, composing guest postings can produce traffic on your site. Guest posting shows that you are dynamic in your locale, while additionally connecting to your site; more on creating backlinks beneath. To execute a visitor posting procedure, you need to discover a webpage that would be a solid match for your organization, draft a blog entry, and afterwards compose a pitch.

8. Quality Backlinks

To direct people to your site, you need to rank high in web indexes. To rank higher in web crawlers, you should be an expert in your industry. One approach to do that is by gaining quality backlinks. In the event that sites with high position connect to your site, that gives you greater validity.

There are two principal manners by which top notch backlinks can help drive more traffic to a site thus boosting ranking and driving reference traffic. From one perspective, backlinks are one of the main ranking components for each significant web index out there. By continually procuring excellent backlinks from applicable sites, you will improve your rankings in SERP and, subsequently, see a lift in your natural traffic.

9. Video Marketing

It is time to add video marketing to your content strategy. According to a report, video will account for 82% of traffic by 2022. Start implementing video marketing into your strategy as soon as possible because this is the content people are clicking on. You can create video for Instagram or Facebook Stories, live videos, IGTV, Facebook Watch, news feed videos, YouTube, etc.

10. Historical Optimization

Historical optimization is the process we use to update old blog content and generate more traffic and leads. A majority of your monthly blog views and leads come from older posts. Historical optimization is a tactic best-suited for a blog that has been around for several years, because you need to be generating a significant amount of organic search traffic, have built up a critical mass of blog subscribers and social media followers, and you need a sizable repository of old posts at your disposal.

11. Internal Linking

At the point when a guest goes to your blog, you will probably get them to keep perusing on different pages of your site. That is the reason interior connections; the connections to different pages on your site are significant. When guests proceed to different pages of your site they are bound to change over and turn into a brand enthusiast.

12. Community Building

Building a network of brand fans is an extraordinary method to ceaselessly direct people to your site. You can fabricate a Facebook gathering, Twitter Talk, LinkedIn Group, or Quora Space explicitly for your supporters and others in your industry where you make esteem, while likewise connecting back to your site. These types of communities keep you top of mind in your customer's eyes. Plus, it is a great way to engage with your followers and learn more about your audience as they evolve over time.

13. Media Coverages

Acquired media coverage is an extraordinary method to drive brand awareness for your organization and traffic to your site. If your showcasing and advertising groups cooperate, you can produce traffic to your site and make fantastic words of mouth. However, most of the sources nowadays attempt to avoid incorporating backlinks in their accounts that does not imply that a decent story will not drive people back to your site.

Media coverage provides great third-party validation for your company. Stories about new products or services, your company culture, or even industry thought leadership can all be great drivers for a reader who maybe had not heard of your company before and wants to learn more.

14. Social Share Buttons

Social share buttons are links that make it easy for your readers to share your content on social media. When your readers become promoters of your content, your traffic will increase. Ask people to share on social media, create strong content, include quotable content, add multimedia such as images, videos, infographics, etc.

15. CTR Optimization

Once your content is posted and you begin ranking on search engines, make sure people are clicking through to read your posts. Your (Click Through Rate (CTR) measures who clicked on your post and read it against the number of people who viewed the link to your post in total. To get more people to click through and drive traffic to your site, it is important to write compelling and apt meta descriptions and titles. To write quality meta tags that are click-worthy, make sure your titles are short and snappy, and your description leaves visitors wanting more.

16. Content Offers

Content offers, here and there alluded to as lead magnets, are an approach to utilize substance to direct people to your site and produce leads. Content offers change contingent upon what phase of the purchaser's excursion your client is in, however can incorporate online classes, guides, reports, preliminaries, demos, agendas, and the sky is the limit from there.

17. Technical SEO

Technical SEO focuses on the backend of your website to see how the pages are technically set up and organized. Factors include elements like page speed, crawling, indexing, and more. Do not underestimate the power technical SEO changes. Technical SEO results in growing your organic traffic by more than 50% in just one month.

18. Local SEO

If your company is a brick-and-mortar store, local SEO is an important factor to consider. To gather information for local search, search engines rely on signals such as local content, social profile pages, links, and citations to provide the most relevant local results to the user.

19. Voice Search Optimization

Voice search is an increasingly important area in which to rank. In fact, according to a research, 65% of 25- to 49-year-old speak to their voice-enabled devices at least once per day. That is why optimizing your content for voice search is essential. When people use voice search, they speak in full sentences. To optimize for voice search, start researching longer tail keywords. The content you write should answer your audience's questions. Writing quick summaries in your posts make it easier for search engines and smart speakers to find the answer they need.

If you are struggling to get traffic to your website, you are not alone. Implementing the tips above can help you increase your traffic as soon as possible. Once your traffic has started to improve, it is time to think about conversions.

Chapter 5: Communication Funnel

A marketing funnel portrays your client's excursion with you. From the underlying stages when somebody finds out about your business, to the buying stage, showcasing channels map courses to change and beyond. With cautious examination, a marketing funnel tells you what your organization should do to impact customers at specific stages. By assessing your funnels, you can possibly drive more prominent deals, more dependability and increase more grounded brand awareness.

The nuts and bolts of the marketing funnel have remained in the business sector since the 1900s. However, no single model is generally acknowledged by all organizations. Some want to keep their model basic, utilizing the "TOFU-MOFU-BOFU" methodology i.e., the top of the funnel, middle of the funnel and bottom of the funnel which alludes to the highest point of funnel, center of channel, and lower part of funnel as particular components. Others believe that adding loyalty and advocacy stages to the funnel improves the marketing strategy. After all, businesses lose up to $1.6 trillion a year when customers leave them.

Marketing funnels improve the client excursion and make it simpler for organizations to follow. These arrangements map out each phase of their customer's choice cycle and plan the means they need to take in each. A marketing funnel applies to practically any client collaboration. Regardless of whether you are searching for online deals, creating traffic for your physical store or gathering clicks as a member, you need a marketing funnel. The funnel is amazing approach to carry perceivability to each phase of associating with your client.

The greatest advantage of showcasing channels is their quantifiability. Your funnel shows you where you are losing clients, to help you rotate your procedure.

For example, in the event that you lose clients before they actually get to the subsequent stage, you need a superior brand awareness campaign.

Businesses to consumer customers often navigate the funnel alone or with trusted advisors like family and friends. Business to consumer clients may never interact directly with a company representative. Business to business customers have larger, more focused buying groups. Business to business consumers interact directly with sales representatives in the lower stages of the marketing funnel

Since marketing compliments the sales process, we find many business owners and marketing managers benefit from learning how their communication efforts can inform their target audience's buying behaviors. Furthermore, it is hard to align or evaluate your marketing expectations with real-world results if you don't understand the customer experience from beginning to end.

In this funnel, people know that you exist and what you do. It also speaks to audiences who recognize that they have a problem they are looking to solve. Generally, this stage is expensive to invest in and offers little return but it is necessary to create an audience for the rest of the funnel. After all, people cannot buy from you if they do not know you exist.

This funnel houses a smaller audience because those who were aware were weeded out and you are left with the people who do have a need and now need to decide between you and your competitors. It is important to note, you will lose quite a few people in this funnel because of the abundance of options available to buyers and that is okay. You only want truly interested people ready to invest in this stage.

This funnel welcomes an even smaller audience group who are now convinced that your product or service is the one for them and they are buying it. This is where you gain your customers. Your pools of interested buyers are now primed to be brand advocates for your product or service. As such, these people will spread the good news about your product or service. But the Marketing Funnel does not stop there. To continue to grow your customer base, do not neglect to stay in touch after they pay you. Continue to nurture them so when they are in need of another product or service or know someone else who can benefit from your business, your brand name will be a part of their referral conversation. Now that is what we call winning.

One such kind of marketing funnel is the communication funnel that is discussed in pretty detail in the sections below, so let us have a look at what a communication funnel is and how to build one.

5.1 What is a Communication Funnel?

There is a critical term. Marketing professionals who help companies to sell more are familiar with sales funnel. However, marketing professionals also use another one, just as essential, but less known, "communication funnel". Regarding the communication, it is more common to speak about a communication strategy than a communication funnel. It is also less challenging to define the first term than the second. Despite lacking a precise definition, we can characterize the communication funnel:

- Cycle: Just like a business funnel, a communication funnel is a living creature, as well. At the point when a brand chooses to adjust its voice, fluctuate the tone or revamp the style technique. So, communication occurs.

- Excursion: The excursion from the first to the last period of a communication funnel additionally includes a specific change. For instance, a pursuer may enter the funnel searching for a snippet of data and leave it related to the brand esteems.

- Deal: Finally, a communication funnel does not end when the deal closes. All things being equal, communication proceeds through client experience.

A communication funnel is a targeted, pre-planned sequence of information delivered to your target (prospective students) in a friendly, conversational tone. Your communications should be relevant, targeted accurately and delivered at the right frequency to keep your prospective target's attention.

Your funnels can be as sophisticated as your technology allows you, but do not let poor tech be an excuse not to start. There are many brilliantly-designed and executed funnel flows out there that are running through ERPs (Enterprise Resource Planning) and basic mailers. If you do not have communication funnels, we promise you that there is no better use of your time than starting these today. If you want your business' sales process to run as efficiently as possible, you absolutely must get your communication funnel; the process of converting a visitor or browser into a paying customer in the right way.

Some business owners are moving away from the term communication funnel because they think it is too mechanical or simplistic to describe the lead nurturing sequence by which customers move from awareness to purchase.

We think it is still a useful way to describe a complex process and it is a good visual to imagine the entire process from start to finish. Following are the stages of a communication funnel:

1. Need Recognition

Naturally, if an individual does not perceive that he has a need that should be filled; he will not make a buy. All things considered; these requirements can go from handily tackled issues to issues without clear arrangements.

Assume your heater goes out in the center of winter. Your concern is self-evident; you need another heater. What is more? The arrangement is simple that you need to call electronic suppliers in your general vicinity for quotes. However, let us state that you need another vehicle. Would it be advisable for you to search for a vehicle, a conservative vehicle or a medium size car? Considerably even vaguer, in case you are baffled with how much your bookkeeper is charging you to do your business' expenses, you probably will not be acquainted with all the various arrangements, similar to cloud based bookkeeping administrations

If you are maintaining a counseling business, for instance, at that point your customers as of now understand that they are having sure issues around your administration zone like a significant expense for every lead (in case you are in advertising) or scattered spending (in case you are in bookkeeping).

2. Information Search
3.

Recognizing a problem or need that you have is the step that triggers a search for more information. The strategies used to gather information tend to vary based on the size and scope of the purchase. Recognizing that you are hungry, for example, might result in a quick Yelp search for restaurants in your area.

Deciding which provider to use to install a new in ground pool at your home, on the other hand, will involve calling around, reading company reviews, visiting showrooms, and talking with salespeople.

According to a survey, 70% of buyers turn to Google at least two to three times during their search to find out more about their problems, potential solutions, relevant businesses, etc. Many people also turn to social media and forums for recommendations. At this point, they are not looking for promotional content; they are looking to learn more about potential solutions for their need. Here is where you can position yourself as the helpful industry expert with content that helps them.

4. Evaluation of Alternatives

If you are running a marketing services business, you might create content about how to choose a marketing agency, pricing guides, whether a company should go for contract or hire in-house, etc.

5. Purchase Decision

The purchase decision is the natural conclusion of the preceding three stages. The potential customer has determined that they have a problem, investigated their options, decided which one is best for them and now they are getting ready to pull out their wallets.

At this stage, bottom of funnel (BOFU) content can help your potential customers feel confident in their decision to purchase your goods or service. Case study content, showcasing the success of a previous or current customer, is very effective, especially when the case studies are relevant to, and reflect, the lead.

Create case studies with customers that reflect different customer profiles, verticals, business sizes, etc. Now for the bad news.

There are two major factors that can hinder purchases at this stage; negative feedback from fellow customers and the prospect's motivation to accept this feedback.

6. Post Purchase Behavior

The sales process is not done just because a purchase has been made. What happens after the sale is just as important. If your new customers are greeted by a thoughtful onboarding process, personal attention and all the resources they need to use your product successfully, they are more likely to confirm to themselves that they have made the right choice. And when they are confident, they are more likely to pass on their satisfaction to others in the form of recommendations and product endorsements.

If your new customers experience disappointment after their purchase, they are more likely to request refunds, write negative reviews and recommend that others in their social circles purchase from your competitors. There is not much content you can create to help facilitate a good post-purchase experience part from just creating a great product. If you have a great product that solves a problem, post-purchase behavior will take care of itself.

No doubt about it, making a deal and utilizing the cycle depicted above is no simple accomplishment. This is not a task you will finish in one evening. It is an interest that you will need to effectively address as long as your organization is good to go. It is not a simple undertaking, but it is one of the few opportunities you have to drive significant improvements in your efficiency and effectiveness when closing deals

5.2 Build a Communication Funnel Model

Some marketing models are digitally focused while others apply equally to digital and traditional forms of communication. For example, some models are designed specifically for digital marketing. Communication is what makes the world go round. If you cannot communicate effectively in the business world, you are just another ordinary company. Having problems communicating with clients is no reason to give up though; we do not want to see you waive your white flag. We are here to help you reach out and make connections.

For starters, let us go over the basic communication model. The model is a visual representation of how a message goes from sender to receiver. Following are the components of a communication model:

1. Sender

The sender is the person who wants to deliver a message. Pretty self-explanatory.

2. Encode

For a sender to transfer a message, they must first translate the message into symbols for the receiver (the one who receives the message). This means taking thoughts, emotions and images and translating them into something the receiver can understand. These symbols often include:

- words
- pictures
- sounds
- Sense information (e.g., touch or smell).

The process of translating these messages into symbols is called encoding.

3. Message Channel

After encoding the message, it is time to communicate the message to a receiver. To do this, we must pick a channel for the message to go through. The channel is the type of medium used to transmit messages between senders and receivers. Examples of channels are:

- Verbal
- Face-to-face
- Over the telephone
- Written
- Letters
- Newspapers
- Visual Media
- Television
- Photographs

4. Decoder

Once the message is received by someone, it is time for the decoding process. Just like a sender must encode messages to communicate, receivers must sense and interpret the symbols to fully understand the message. They then decode the symbols back into images, emotions and thoughts to make sense of them.

5. Receiver

The receiver is the person who receives the message.

Now that you know all of the steps of the communication process, it can easily be connected.

When messages are decoded exactly as the sender has intended, the sender and receiver have matching perceptions of the message being communicated. When everyone is on the same page, effective communication occurs.

We need to remember that everybody is unique. Individuals vary in their own chronicles, which gives them various encounters and enthusiastic reactions to your message. This leads to difference in the manner messages are encoded, sent, gotten and perceived. Individuals connect various implications to the words, pictures, sounds and signals utilized during correspondence dependent on past encounters.

A purchaser persona is a semi-anecdotal portrayal of your optimal client dependent on statistical surveying and genuine information about your current clients. This incorporates client socioeconomics, standards of conduct, inspirations and objectives. The more detailed, the better. Purchaser personas will help figure out where to center your time and guide item improvement, which brings about the capacity to draw in the most significant guests, leads and clients to your business.

These buyer personas are like pure gold for your marketing. You need to hit your target audience, and buyer personas will give you a clear idea of how you can reach each demographic. Keeping in mind everyone is different; remember their preferred way to intake information is different as well. Some people are visual learners; some are kinesthetic, while others may prefer audio. Reach these different audiences by using multiple message channels. Radio, TV, print and web can all be utilized effectively once you understand your buyer persona. After reviewing buyer personas, we can build websites including text, photos, videos, or podcasts based on the preferred communication style of the receiver.

As you are encoding and customizing the message channel to learning styles, envision you are having a discussion with every purchaser persona. For instance, if your crowd is a group of little children, short simple words will work incredible. For your grandmother, the words can be further developed and possibly have a higher volume or bigger textual style contingent upon your medium. For the two groups, you might need to consider a bigger book size for simple reading. Consider your purchaser persona, how they will unravel your message and how to best prevail upon them utilizing this data.

Since you have caught the consideration of your objective beneficiaries, there might be a reach in interests inside that gathering. This is when fragmenting proves to be useful. Once more, it is about personalization-consider your purchaser persona. Individuals would prefer not to be overwhelmed with data they could not care less about. By chance if you plan on conveying advertisement sheets with coupons, you are not going to send school matured understudies' coupons for buying clothes. That age bunch in all probability could not care less about that item and that advertisement is no doubt going in the waste.

You can make numerous advertisements that appeal to the various purchasers and send them to the various fragments you have inside your crowd. Now that you know the process of communication, use it to your advantage. The basic communication model allows communicators to really think about how they are going to get their point across at the most basic levels. Keep in mind the differences between people and use a channel that is most appropriate for your receivers. You are now ready to communicate with clients.

5.3 Variables of a Successful Online Campaign to Grow Your Company

There are countless things to consider, similar to whether the office can really convey on their guarantees or in the event that they will deplete your money consistently with no return. Moreover, whenever you have limited it down to a couple of competitors, you may think about what a sensible cost for a decent organization is, or whether you even need one in any case. Following are some variables that are important for a successful online campaign to grow your company:

1. Your Branding

Your logo configuration, shading plan and straplines should connect with and interest your clients to urge them to pick your brand over your rivals. In the event that your brand does not make the correct impression, you can refresh your organization logo through rebranding or by introducing your brand in another manner through a publicizing effort. Branding is something which is often overlooked in small businesses but when you are clear about what your business stands for and how you want to be perceived, your consumers will get the message. If it is unclear, then they will be unclear why they should work with you.

2. Search Engine Optimization

Site improvement is a critical method to boost your site presentation on web sites like Google. At the point when your site has incredible SEO, you will show high up in the natural indexed lists in Google. At a fundamental level, SEO is tied in with guaranteeing that you have a substance rich site with all around upgraded pages, and loads of inbound connections and social offers. The web is a serious spot, and without extraordinary SEO it is extremely hard to get enough traffic to accomplish elevated levels of enquiries and deals.

3. Experience

You should ensure that you have experience of planning and running some bit of advertising efforts. The exact opposite thing you need is to go through many months on content creation or a large number of dollars on paid traffic just to see no positive outcomes and have no clue about where you turned out wrong.

It takes time to satisfy all these criteria. It is difficult to post high-quality content every single day when you have a bunch of other pressing business issues on your plate. It is not easy to craft an airtight process to help new hires hit the ground running from day one. It is just a fact of life that there is going to be some trial and error involved.

But if you hire a digital marketing agency, you can avoid the cost of trial and error of running your own campaigns, getting your team up to speed, spending time and company resources on maintaining your content consistency, and so forth. You can also avoid getting sidetracked from other important things you have to do, like closing deals or getting investors.

4. Your Understanding of Your Target Market

Each advertising procedure has an objective market that you need to reach. Regardless of whether you are not sure who you should target, start by contributing data that you do know. Sorting out the demographics of your intended interest group is an incredible spot to begin. When you are certain about the demographics, you will need to make a purchaser's persona.

The purchaser's persona is the distinct advantage utilized by effective advertising organizations.

The purchaser's persona incorporates data; things such as age, sexual orientation, and pay. Contingent upon your necessities, it can incorporate subtleties like what they appreciate eating, the number of children they have, or even what sports groups they cheer for.

The fact of the matter is that you need to comprehend your objective market, so you know where you can target them, how they carry on, and what sort of interests they have. If by chance you do not comprehend your objective market you cannot in any way, shape or form hope to contact them.

5. Watching the Data

Use a free marketing data tool, there is no excuse for not keeping a close eye on the data. With the availability of marketing data, companies can track which web pages are generating the most clicks, how long visitors are staying on pages, where site visitors are coming from, and much, much more. Failure to spend the time needed to watch data can mean the failure of the entire marketing strategy.

6. Communicating the Value to Your Customers

The most impressive marketing strategies in the world will not work unless you communicate the value of your product or service to your customers. You need to clearly communicate exactly what your product offers. If they can purchase a similar good or service elsewhere, you need to communicate what makes yours different and better than your competitor.

7. Enthusiasm

Keep in mind the intensity of enthusiasm in any undertaking. In the event that you give it a second thought or could not care less about a venture, it will show in the eventual outcome.

Regardless of whether you are selling a hair care item or bananas, you should be enthusiastic about your organization, your item or administration, and your promoting methodology. Business is a drawn-out speculation where you need to locate a solid inspiration toward the start. By chance if you do not have energy at the start, you will always be unable to keep it going over the long period.

In the long run, your absence of energy will show itself, regardless of whether in the nature of the item, the absence of bearing in your showcasing effort, or in the manner in which you handle client communications via web-based media and online discussions. Basically expressed, individuals can enlighten when an organization does not mind regarding its clients, and in the end, they will become quite mindful, as well.

8. Focus

The best companies out there focus on helping customers, not on making money. It is not an intuitive idea, the thought of putting customers ahead of profits, but it works. As soon as your company starts focusing on giving value to customers, there is an almost organic growth that occurs that is almost inexplicable. The practice of placing more value on money rather than the human component sabotages any kind of effort you make to grow your business. Good businesses do not just work that way. To achieve this kind of focus, be sure to include your marketing team on meetings and find other ways your company can add value to people's lives. This will help remind your marketing team of the real mission of the business.

The above variables are all extremely important for success of any company in the online world.

5.4 Building an Attractive Character Online

With regards to individual marking, an attractive character begins with you and the capacity to pull in individuals to you by sharing your very own accounts. You can turn into an attractive character to get individuals to know you, similar to you, need to gain from you, confide in you and in the long run work with you by sharing your very own accounts to rouse and charm your crowd.

The way to building your attractive character is to comprehend that individuals will follow you since you have finished the excursion they are on the present moment, and they need the outcomes you have just accomplished. Turning into an attractive character is an extremely ground-breaking methodology with regards to building your own image and composing a business channel or a duplicate. At the point when you make an attractive character for your business channel that everybody is attracted to, they will almost be certain about work with you.

An attractive character will be utilized for all that you will do, identified with building your online presence, which will prompt the deals of your items and administrations. An attractive character will likewise rouse and persuade your crowd to make a monstrous move.

Individuals will be attracted to you as an attractive character since you are addressing their trouble spots, issues, and through their encounters. They will be pulled in to you more than you will acknowledge on the grounds that you will be driving with esteem.

This is the reason it is significant for you to be genuine, straightforward and powerless. Your crowd is more intrigued to know how you made your progress. They need to know your story, your excursion, your battles and by you imparting your story to them, they will be enlivened in the light of the fact that you are telling them that you are much the same as them.

The principal component is that your character needs to have a type of handle. A handle is fundamentally your slogan. A slogan is genuinely imperative to many individuals in brand advertising. It is a decent route for individuals to identify with you, regardless of whether your handle is basically something you use when you are marking your messages. What you choose for your handle is your decision, yet customarily it will rely on what merchandise or administrations you are attempting to advance.

The second important element in creating an attractive character is to include some type of back story for the character. Customers who are buying your products or services want results. If you can share a back story of how you or your customers have received the results that your potential customers seek, they will instantly be attracted and will relate to you and your company.

The third component of building an appealing character is character. Remember individual subtleties for the messages you send, discourses you give, conversations you have before a crowd of people, or in any sort of promoting or advertising effort. It is critical to mesh individual stories into your correspondences paying little heed to their structure. The more noteworthy the assortment of alluring characters you can use in your advertising, the more prominent the assortment of individuals you can pull in to your business.

Many individuals feel that character defects are something awful to admit to or share. In the event that you take a look at any great superhuman, any great comic book legend, any great film, the primary characters consistently have imperfections. This is vital, on the grounds that it makes them human. People will better relate to somebody who is not great. They will need to hear you out.

Similarly, it is additionally alright to show your quirks, your annoyances, even your solid feelings. One thing that the vast majorities fear when they are sharing their own accounts as a component of their showcasing is insulting somebody. It is more critical to understand that lack of bias is exhausting. At the point when you are unbiased, no one tunes in to you.

When you are questionable or forceful, or when you have a position or convictions or assessments and you share those things, not every person will concur with you, but rather it will draw in more individuals to you. You might be asking yourself how you can share these components as a feature of your alluring character. Share them through messages, instant messages, and other marketing interchanges.

You make an attractive character when settling on the back story, character imperfections, and solid suppositions that you are willing to share. Continuously remember that extremity is acceptable; lack of bias is exhausting. Start making your appealing character with a decent back story and mesh it into the entirety of the showcasing that you do.

Conclusion

Web-based Media has been of incredible assistance to a significant number of people living in your environmental factors. In the event that you investigate the general public today that we live in, we can undoubtedly perceive how web-based media has made numerous typical looking people transform into stars. It can truly flip around your life on the off chance that you begin to utilize it effectively. Today, web-based media is not simply bound to Facebook or Twitter. Today, online media contains numerous applications that you can use to succeed. Also, interestingly, every web-based media application has its own intended interest group and each needs an alternate kind of treatment to help you succeed.

This book is all about growing your company online in a successful way. Growing your company online may look very difficult to you because currently, you may think who would even consider you for any sort of thing, but trust me the online world is the king of all. Mastering the online tricks and tips to succeed, you can easily become the best in the game. With this amazing knowledge regarding marketing by your side, nothing is impossible anymore. Within, the span of a couple of months of hard work and should we change the thought of "hard work" to "smart work" you can become the best in town.

In this book, we have given you a detailed outlook on the importance of sales funnel, the different building blocks of sales funnels available to you presently and what actually is a sales funnel. Growing your company online is a pretty easy job with the correct information and appropriate tools. You can even effectively manage your sales funnel with the detailed information that has been given in the chapters above.

Success has been the talk of the book; you can start earning with the help of online growth of your company. You can start making a value ladder for your business and see how effectively your business grows in a couple of months. You will also learn the importance of value ladder and the benefits that come along with a value ladder. You will also learn the term online traffic in this book and the techniques of increasing the online traffic to your company's website.

Well, it is pretty clear; master the art of online growth you will find success at your door step. Do not wait any further, it is your time to succeed, so start branding but start growing online in the right way using this book as your best partner.